THE TRANSFORMATION OF THE PUBLIC SECTOR: THE ROLE OF ACCOUNTING IN SUSTAINING CHANGE

Irvine Lapsley
with
Tom Brown
Audrey Jackson
Rosie Oldfield
Chris Pong

University of Edinburgh

Published by
The Institute of Chartered Accountants of Scotland

First published 2003
The Institute of Chartered Accountants of Scotland

©2003
ISBN 1 871250 96 X

Printed and bound in Great Britain by
Antony Rowe Ltd., Chippenham, Wiltshire

657.83500941 LAP

020074808

RESEARCH REPORTS
REFEREEING PROCESS

The Research Committee applies a rigorous refereeing process to all stages of its research reports. The refereeing process operates by sending the initial research proposal to two independent referees (one academic and one practitioner). The academic referee will either be a member of the Panel listed below or an *ad hoc* referee. All proposals are also reviewed by the Director of Research who remains in close contact with the project. The two referees are consulted on the academic and technical standard of the draft research report. In particular, they are asked to comment on:

- the academic rigour of the document;
- the validity of the approach taken in the report;
- whether the presentation of the report identifies the key issues and brings these to the attention of the intended reader; and
- whether the document will add to the knowledge and understanding of the interested reader.

Professor J Broadbent	Royal Holloway, University of London
Professor R H Gray	University of Glasgow
Professor J Haslam	Heriot-Watt University
Professor J Holland	University of Glasgow
Professor T Lee	University of Dundee
Professor W M McInnes	University of Stirling
Professor S McLeay	University of Wales
Professor H Mellett	Cardiff University
Professor M J Page	University of Portsmouth
Professor C Roberts	University of Aberdeen
Professor M J Sherer	University of Essex
Professor R Taffler	Cranfield University
Professor P Weetman	University of Strathclyde
Professor R M S Wilson	University of Loughborough

The Research Committee is grateful to all those who participate in the refereeing process.

CONTENTS

CONTENTS

GLOSSARY OF TERMS AND ABBREVIATIONS

Activity Based Costing: An approach to the costing and monitoring of activities which involves tracing consumption and costing final outputs. Resources are assigned to activities and activities to costs objects based on consumption estimates. The latter utilise cost drivers to attach activity costs to outputs.

Activity Based Management: A system of management which uses activity-based cost information for a variety of purposes including cost reduction, cost modelling and customer profitability analysis.

Balanced Scorecard: An approach to the provision of information to management to assist strategic policy formulation and achievement. It emphasises the need to provide the user with a set of information which addresses all relevant areas of performance in an objective and unbiased fashion. The information provided may include both financial and non-financial elements and cover areas such as profitability, customer satisfaction, internal efficiency and innovation.

Compulsory Competitive Tendering (CCT): A process whereby public service providers put part of their services out to tender and in which in-house providers compete against private sector operators to determine the most economical manner of service provision.

Functional Cost Analysis: An analysis of the relationships between product functions, their perceived value to the customer and their cost of provision.

Key Performance Indicators (KPI): Financial and non-financial measures of the most important aspects of business performance.

Private Finance Initiative (PFI): Mechanism for providing funds for the acquisition of assets by public sector organisations without these organisations incurring debt.

Public Private Partnerships (PPP): Collaborative ventures between private sector financiers and public sector providers. Successor to Private Finance Initiative (PFI).

Resource Management: A budgeting system which combines financial estimates with non-financial indicators of workload and quality.

Strategic Cost Management: The application of cost management techniques so that they simultaneously improve the strategic position of the firm and reduce costs.

Target Costing: Estimating product costs by establishing a competitive market price based on cost reductions made possible by the improvement of technologies and processes.

Value for Money (VFM): economy, efficiency and effectiveness.

Zero Based Budgeting: A method of budgeting which requires each cost element to be specifically justified, as though the activities to which the budget relates were being undertaken for the first time.

FOREWORD

When the Research Committee of The Institute of Chartered Accountants of Scotland decided, some years ago, to allocate a substantial lump sum to support accounting research in the public sector, it did so because it was evident that chartered accountants could and should contribute to the recognised need for ongoing transformation in that sector.

This research study is one of the principal outcomes of that funding commitment[1]. The picture it shows is not a happy one. It suggests that transformation is not being achieved by the budgeting process, or by the application of value-for-money (VFM) techniques nor by the introduction of major IT projects nor by the use of consultants, although those processes and initiatives can support transformation.

The study also shows that the relatively crude mechanisms employed by the Treasury, namely enforced real cost reductions, have been a powerful and effective driver for transformation, by focussing senior management attention on effectiveness and in identifying relevant key performance indicators. It shows, too, that accrual based accounting has already changed the management culture.

No-one would have expected transformation to be easy not least because the complexity of objectives in the public sector is greater than is typical in the private sector. An increasing focus on output measures, as well as on input measures is an important part of this. The established tools available include VFM reviews, which itself include output related assessment as part of the effectiveness element. So it is important that VFM techniques are not eclipsed or overlooked in the search for techniques that work.

---

[1] The other report funded by this commitment *From Bureaucracy to Responsive Management:A Comparative Study of Local Government Change* was published by ICAS in 2002.

ICAS hopes that in sponsoring this research it will have made a useful contribution to the urgent need to find transformation techniques and approaches that work. There are no easy answers here and the continuing need to make a given level of the gross national product achieve more, each year, suggests that the issue will remain one of central importance to the nation as well as to those with direct management responsibility in the public sector.

Nigel Macdonald
Convener
Research Committee

May 2003

ACKNOWLEDGMENTS

In undertaking this project, the researchers have been grateful for the co-operation of all those who were interviewed, who took part in group discussions or who completed surveys. This research strategy has resulted in a comprehensive picture of key aspects of the transformation of the public sector.

This research has been undertaken by a group of researchers at the Institute of Public Sector Accounting Research at the University of Edinburgh. Chapters one, two, three and nine were contributed by Irvine Lapsley. Chapter four was contributed by Chris Pong with Irvine Lapsley. Chapter five was contributed by Tom Brown. Chapters six and seven were contributed by Irvine Lapsley and Rosie Oldfield. Chapter eight was contributed by Audrey Jackson with Irvine Lapsley.

This research has benefited greatly from presentation of interim ideas and papers at a variety of places. This includes the European Accounting Association Annual Congress, Munich (2000) and Athens (2001), the Irish Accounting and Finance Association Conference in Dublin (2000), and a conference in Edinburgh in June 2001 which was hosted by The Institute of Chartered Accountants of Scotland. It also included plenary presentations by Irvine Lapsley at a conference to celebrate the 25th anniversary of the regional government of Andalucia in Seville, December 2001 and at an international conference on Public Sector Accounting in Tokyo, February 2002. The authors acknowledge the helpful comments of the anonymous reviewers.

EXECUTIVE SUMMARY

Introduction

The UK public sector has been transformed over the past few decades. In an increasingly global economy, the main lever by which central governments can influence the success of the domestic economy is by ensuring its public sector operates efficiently. The central governments of the developed economies have adopted similar change agendas to transform their public sectors. These change agendas entail the introduction of new structures, new kinds of organisations and a 'reinvention' of many parts of the public sector. The intention of successive governments has been the creation of a 'New Public Sector', which is more strategic and corporate in its thinking, with a customer/service user focus. This 'New Public Sector' is intended to replace a public sector characterised by bureaucracy, professionalism and departmentalism. The scope of the reforms is so extensive both across the public sector and within sub-sectors, such as health and local government, that not all aspects of public sector change are included in this study. The outputs of the public sector are also notoriously difficult to measure. Therefore, we have narrowed the focus of this research to take a distinct accounting angle. Specifically this research is concerned with (1) the role of accounting in effecting such changes and (2) the actual and likely impact of such changes on public sector accountants themselves.

The approach adopted

Given the complexity of the changes being introduced across the public sector, this research study proceeded by: (1) identifying key mechanisms with which accountants would be expected to be involved as devices for bringing about change; and (2) seeking the views of accountants on actual and likely impacts of such changes on their duties and responsibilities. This research involved a combined approach, with varying methods being deployed for different dimensions of the study.

The four mechanisms identified as key change drivers were: (1) budgets, (2) VFM audits, (3) major IT initiatives and (4) management consultants. Each of these mechanisms for change was investigated in different ways: (1) budgets were investigated by the use of case studies of practices in the NHS and local government in Scotland; (2) VFM audits were investigated by exploring the experiences of an expert group of VFM auditors; (3) major IT initiatives were examined by scrutiny of reports, government studies and meetings in the public domain; and (4) management consultants were interviewed to obtain their perspective on changes in practice in the public sector.

In addition to these investigations of how accountants are implicated in changes in the public sector, we sought to assess the impact of public sector reforms on accountants in two ways, firstly, by obtaining the views of an expert group of leading figures in the public sector on how public sector reforms were impacting on the skills and competencies of public sector accountants and secondly, by a survey of accountants working in the public sector to ascertain the adoption of innovations in accounting techniques to support the new, managerial public sector.

Key findings: Mechanisms of change

1. Budgets

This study examined the operation of budgets in two settings: (1) the NHS and (2) local government, using case studies of experiences in Scotland. We summarise the key findings on this dimension of the study:

NHS

It has long been recognised that the key decision makers on the use of health care resources are clinicians. Over the past two decades there have been numerous initiatives to devise budgetary systems which integrate clinicians into formal management structures in hospitals. There is an extensive literature which demonstrates that these initiatives on clinical budgeting have not worked as intended. In this study, we reported upon 'successful' clinical budgeting systems *ie* ones which connect with clinicians and in which medical professionals with administrative responsibilities act upon budgetary information.

Key Finding (1): clinical budgets are often depicted as constraints on the implementation of management and organisational change in the NHS. This study has shown that this need not be the case. A longitudinal study of clinical budgeting has detected effective systems of budgeting whose operational effectiveness depends mainly on the manner and timing of their introduction and a holistic approach to their design.

Local Government

The budget is often regarded as the central feature of local government management. It has a key role in the allocation of resources across the various services which comprise local authorities. Traditionally, local authority budgeting has operated on the basis of a projection of forward spending plans for one year only, which is closely related to previous patterns of expenditure, with incremental changes. This has been modified with the introduction of three year budgeting. Findings in the local government case studies supported the view that the budget was an important mechanism within local authorities, but that it was a 'blunt instrument'.

Key Finding (2): Budgets within local government are change mechanisms. However, financial information could be linked more effectively to policy options to enhance the quality of information and to make budgets more than 'blunt instruments' for the implementation of change programmes.

2. *VFM Audits*

VFM is a significant component of both the thinking behind, and the practice for, reforming the practices of public sector institutions. In terms of the policies towards the transformation of the UK's public sector, the VFM concept can be seen as the unifying mechanism and as the most important device deployed by accountants in securing public sector change. In this study, the practice and effectiveness of VFM was explored by seeking the views of an expert group of VFM auditors. This evidence confirmed the importance of VFM, but it also pointed to its limits. In particular, VFM auditors had undertaken the more obvious studies and now faced very challenging VFM studies.

Key Finding (3): VFM audit is, and has been, a key change mechanism in reforming the public sector. However, the maturity of VFM as a technique means that there is a need for clarification of what constitutes best practice in high level VFM audits. Also, within the context of the Best Value regime, there is a need for oversight bodies to review the role of VFM.

3. *IT initiatives*

Accountants are frequently involved in IT initiatives within the public sector on a variety of levels: whether in the procurement process; in the implementation of such systems; in the screening of potential IT strategies; in advising organisations on appropriate

IT strategies; or as the custodian of IT developments within public sector organisations. This important role for accountants in IT developments was examined in the context of the government's vision of a public sector which would be transformed in its service delivery by IT initiatives. In this study, an entire raft of such IT initiatives are explored, which demonstrate that the complexity of the public sector has defeated systems designers.

Key Finding (4):The vision of a public sector transformed by a series of high level IT initiatives has proved unfounded. Of particular interest to financial managers at the highest levels of the public sector are the weaknesses of procurement policy and of project management.

4. *Management consultants*

Management consultants are widely credited with a major influence on the implementation of reforms in the public sector. The services provided by these management consultants have often been by consultancy firms which are part of, or associated with, accounting practices. This part of this study investigated the impact of such consultancies from the perspective of the management consultants themselves. However, it revealed a story of frustrations on the part of management consultants. Often their terms of reference were very specific, and frequently they were just used as an extra resource. Frequently when they were asked to investigate situations, these management consultants said their reports were not acted upon.

Key Finding (5): Depicting management consultants as a major factor in changing the public sector is suspect. Their major preoccupation is with making specific technologies work, but not in transforming public sector institutions. There is a need for a major VFM study on the use of management consultants in the public sector.

Key findings: The accountant in the 'New Public Sector'

In addition to examining the impact of change mechanisms and the role of accountants and accounting in informing change, this study explored the effect of the public sector reforms on accountants. The particular focus on this part of this study was on the kind of skills and competencies which the accountants would require to be a success in a transformed public sector (The 'New Public Sector'). This aspect of this study gathered data in two ways: (1) by obtaining the views of the members of an expert group of leading public sector accountants, eminent members of the UK accounting profession, with significant experience of major changes in their own industries or organisations and with large numbers of finance personnel in their organisations; and (2) a survey of accountants within the public sector to determine the extent of the use and the spread of new techniques of accounting which might be expected to be deployed in the new managerial public sector.

The findings of the discussions with members of the expert group confirm that the public sector has been experiencing significant change in its operations and environment. In their view these changes have important consequences, not only for the skills and competencies of present day public sector accountants but also for the public sector accountant of the future.

Key Finding (6): In the view of the expert group, the traditional role of 'regularity' was likely to decline in the future. The public sector accountant of the future would have a role which would be more strategic and entrepreneurial. This has major implications for public sector employers and for the professional accounting bodies.

For the survey, key innovations in accounting practice were identified. This included ABC, ABM and the Balanced Scorecard. The findings from this survey are summarised in Key Finding 7.

Key Finding (7): Regulatory forces are the main determinants of accounting innovation in the public sector. The principal focus of change has been on performance measurement. There is little evidence of experimentation with novel accounting techniques in the public sector, based on this survey.

Conclusion

In the past two decades, the public sector has undergone a period of persistent change. This is beyond dispute. The present study has sought to clarify the influence of accounting and accountants as agents of change within the reform of the public sector. Within the public sector accounting literature there is often a presumption that accounting is of fundamental importance to reform. This report presents evidence of a more subtle role.

Within the conventional array of accounting practices, the budget is often seen as a powerful tool for change in the public sector. This research makes two points: (1) budgetary practices have greater potential for change than the prevailing wisdom on hospital budgeting suggests; and (2) while the budget is powerful in local government, there is a need for greater sophistication of approach to link costs, outcomes and policy options. We also note that VFM is arguably the most significant mechanism of change in the public sector reform, but it may be approaching the limits of its use. Furthermore, mechanisms which have depicted as significant agencies of change (management consultants) or which have expected to significantly change the public sector (IT developments) have been less influential in bringing about sustainable change in the public sector.

The manner in which accounting, and accountants, will have a significant role in initiating and sustaining change in the public sector will depend mainly on the acquisition of new skills and competencies. The public sector accountant of the future will not slavishly follow accounting practices which emanate from the private sector and will be more strategic in his or her thinking and more entrepreneurial in his or her behaviour.

CHAPTER ONE

INTRODUCTION

This research is an examination of firstly, the role of accounting in effecting and sustaining changes in the public sector and secondly, the actual and likely impact of such changes on public sector accountants themselves, and their ability to sustain changes in the public sector.

The context of this study is the consistent aim of successive governments to reform the public sector and, in the process, create a 'New Public Sector'. This 'New Public Sector' is intended to be more strategic in its thinking, more efficient in its behaviour and more responsive to the needs of citizens or customers. It would supplant traditional practices and procedures which have often been characterised as overly bureaucratic, inefficient and inward-looking with the interests of major professional groupings dominating policies and practices of public sector organisations. In the pursuit of a transformed public sector, the breadth and scope of the reforms to the public sector over the past couple of decades has been wide-ranging (including, for example, the privatisation of utilities; the attempt to introduce the internal market in health care; and the introduction of new forms of organisation, such as Hospital Trusts in the NHS, Direct Service Organisations in local government and Next Steps agencies and the Financial Management Initiative in central government).

Many of the aforementioned reforms were introduced by the reforming Conservative governments from 1979 onwards. However, the Labour administrations of 1997 and 2001 have also been intent on changing the public sector, under the banner of modernisation. This has resulted in continuity of certain policies which were introduced by the Conservative administrations (for example, the retention of hospital trusts and direct service organisations; and the redesigning of the Private

Finance Initiative as Public-Private Partnerships), but also new policies which were designed to improve the public sector. Notable examples of such new policies introduced by the Labour Government include the introduction of Best Value in local government, the establishment of the National Institute for Clinical Excellence and the Commission for Health Improvement in the NHS.

The research strategy adopted in this study has not been the compilation of a descriptive account of all the accounting changes which have flowed from these reforms to the public sector. Instead, we have identified key mechanisms in initiating and sustaining changes to the public sector and analysed their impact. The specific mechanisms studied here were (1) the budget, (2) VFM audit, (3) IT initiatives and (4) the use of management consultants.

Of these change mechanisms, the budget is widely regarded as the principal tool for levering change in public sector organisations. However, despite this apparent power as a change mechanism, there have been many attempts to reform its use in the NHS and local government and, most recently, in central government, with the introduction of Resource Accounting and Budgeting. The reforms in central government are still in their infancy, so this study concentrates on the NHS and local government. The second of these change mechanisms, VFM, can be seen as one of the most important devices deployed by accountants in securing public sector change. Its constituent elements of economy, efficiency and effectiveness are now embedded in the everyday language of the public sector in evaluations of changes, whether of strategic importance or of an operational nature. The third change mechanism, IT initiatives, has been an important part of public sector reforms for some time, but has been given a fresh impetus in the current government's modernisation policies. This particular change mechanism is of importance to public sector accountants on a variety of levels including project management; and stewardship responsibilities for the IT function in organisations, which included procurement policies, implementation strategies and the screening of potential IT systems. Finally, the use of management consultants is also selected as a change mechanism. The role of management consultants in effecting change in the public sector has been the subject of considerable discussion. The link to accountants has a number of dimensions: many of the most important management consultancies have or have had links to accounting firms. Also, within public sector organisations, there are many examples of management consultants being hired to implement accounting systems; often accountants within public sector organisations have significant roles in the procurement of management consultants to ensure value for money is achieved.

The impact of these change mechanisms are assessed against Costello's (1994) classification of change states in organisations. Costello classifies changes in three categories:

1. *Developmental*

   • This is changing the organisation by the introduction of a new technology or specific management practice.

2. *Transitional*

   • This is the introduction of new techniques, methods, procedures or services which lead to the introduction of new structures and the reorganisation of the entity.

3. *Transformational*

   • This is the introduction or the evolution of a new structure which also results in a change in the organisational strategy and vision.

Of these change states, transformational is the desired state for the creation of a 'New Public Sector' by the reformers of successive governments in the UK. An *ex ante* appraisal of the impact of the change mechanisms discussed above against these three change states identified by Costello (*op. cit.*) is shown in table 1.1. This desired state is evidenced by the number, scale and frequency of reforms over the past two decades, by the consistent pattern of reform towards what is called a 'New Public Sector' as evidenced by the importance of management, of performance and of accounting in both informing management and measuring performance. This desired state is also supported by studies which support the contention that accounting information and mechanisms have a central role in the transformation of the public sector (Olson *et al*, 1998; Guthrie *et al*, 1999; Pollitt and Bouckaert, 2000).

Table 1.1   *Change States and Change Mechanisms: Ex Ante Appraisal*

Change State \ Change Mechanism	(1) Budgets	(2) VFM	(3) IT	(4) Management Consultants
1. Developmental	√	√	√	√
2. Transitional	√	√	√	√
3. Transformational	-	√	√	√

In addition to locating the impact of these change mechanisms in the context of Costello's change states framework, this study goes on to examine the experiences and practices of accountants in the public sector. There are two parts to this aspect of this study, firstly, an examination of the skills and competencies which the public sector accountant of the future will require; and secondly, a survey of the adoption of innovations in accounting practice by accountants in the public sector. These issues are discussed in chapters seven and eight. This approach provides a distinctive analysis of the actual and future role of accountants in the implementation and sustaining of public sector reforms.

CHAPTER TWO

THE APPROACH ADOPTED

This research into the transformation of the UK public sector has drawn on a variety of sources – a combined research strategy to produce as authoritative a view as possible of what is happening and has happened in its reform. There is an established literature (see Smith, 1975; Denzin, 1978; Brewer and Hunter, 1989) on the use of combined methods of research investigation. The essence of the combined approach is based on scepticism of the validity of results when a single method (*eg* survey, model-building, archival searches) is used. Instead, proponents of the combined approach advocate more than one method to corroborate results. This advocacy of the combined approach is particularly relevant, as in this study, where complex phenomena with multiple dimensions are under investigation. This study is in two parts: (1) examination of change mechanisms; and (2) an investigation of how public sector changes impact on accountants. As regards (1), change mechanisms, this study has entailed:

- field studies at different study settings;
- expert groups to gain an in-depth knowledge of specific accounting practices;
- the scrutiny and analysis of documents; and
- surveys.

The researchers in this team have undertaken a variety of field studies. There have been case studies of hospitals at the leading edge of innovations in budgeting (Lapsley, 2001a) and case studies of local governments in the face of significant modernisation agendas from central government and oversight agencies (Lapsley and Pallot, 2000). The researchers have also used the technique of expert groups to investigate VFM Audit (Lapsley and Pong, 2000). In the investigation of IT initiatives as a mechanism of change, the researchers have drawn on publicly available documents and reports which had previously not been analysed in a consistent fashion (Brown, 2001). This approach has also been adopted in exploring the connections between the change programmes of the Thatcher government (and its successor) and the modernisation agenda of the 'New' Labour administration of 1997 onwards (Lapsley, 2001b). The researchers have also used surveys and interviewed key actors in the transformation of the public sector – management consultants (Lapsley and Oldfield, 2001a). Overall, these various studies have entailed interviews with 126 budget holders, finance staff and other specialists in the field of the UK public sector.

The investigation of part (2) of the study, the impact of public sector accounting changes on accountants working in the public sector was undertaken in two stages. First, the views of an expert group of leading practitioners within the finance function in the public sector were obtained (Lapsley and Oldfield, 2000, 2001b). Second, a survey was undertaken of accountants working in the public sector to determine the extent to which changes in the public sector accounting were accompanied by innovations in accounting practices.

CHAPTER THREE

ROLE OF BUDGETS

The budget has long been accepted as a key instrument of change in the public sector. Indeed, Henley *et al* (1992) describe the significance of the budget in public sector organisations in the following terms:

> *In many ways, the annual budget is the central component of management accounting in public sector organisations. In part, this is a reflection of the environment in which public service organisations operate with an emphasis on the short term, particularly the fiscal year. In this scenario, the annual budget becomes the dominant management tool for planning, co-ordinating, organising and controlling activities.*

While the budget in public sector organisations has often been criticised because it has been based on historical patterns of expenditure, with incremental changes from year to year, it nevertheless affords the opportunity to scrutinise the deployment of all the organisation's resources and to make changes in line with policy reviews.

However, the importance of the budget as a mechanism which can achieve change which extends beyond 'developmental' to 'transitional' or 'transformational' (Costello, 1994) has come under attack in recent years by the proponents of 'beyond budgeting'. The 'beyond budgeting' trend has emerged from the world of practice, from the private sector in Scandinavia, with Wallander (1999) as its original proponent. The Wallander critique is based on the idea that in budget construction the underlying assumptions are critical: if your assumptions are that things will continue or there may be marginal adjustments, there is no need for a budget. However, even if the assumptions underlying your budget are based on radical change, Wallander's critique is that the budget will not show this. In addition what is necessary is information about what people are doing right now; the figures should be action-oriented; targets should be set in benchmarking mode; and there should be continuous forecasting. Bearing in mind these criticisms of the significance of budgets as instruments of policy change and implementation the researchers have studied the use of budgets within the UK public sector, specifically in the National Health Service (NHS) and local government. These studies are based on case studies of budgeting experiences.

Case study experiences: (1) the NHS

In many ways, the UK's NHS fits the Wallander critique. One distinct kind of hospital budgeting – clinical budgeting – has been subject to study which demonstrates *failure*, which is taken here as the inability of these systems to generate information which is regarded as meaningful by the target recipients and which they therefore do not act upon in the discharge of their duties. There are a variety of reasons for this *failure*. This includes power struggles between doctors and administrators. This is exacerbated by the existence of 'decoupled organisations': doctors in one culture and administrators in another. There is evidence of resistance by hospital doctors to cost containment initiatives, and rejection by doctors of the idea of being expected to use accounting information. There has also been a failure to integrate doctors in hospital management and in a way that they retain the trust of their colleagues. An outcome has been the 'fabrication' of budgets in the uncertainty of what they should be. Also operational difficulties have been observed in making different parts of hospitals work in concert to support clinical budgeting systems.

Against this history of accounting failure, there is a success story in which success is measured as an operational clinical budgeting system which budget holders act on (Lapsley, 2001a). This was a longitudinal study of two case study hospital sites targeted for the introduction of two forms of clinical budgeting: (1) management budgeting; and

(2) resource management. One of these sites was chosen because it had particularly good IT resources (see chapter 5). Both of these sites were selected for support from management consultants (see chapter 6). At these two case study sites it was found that the initial reform – management budgeting – was a failure at both sites, *ie* this system just did not function as intended. There were a number of reasons for this failure. There was some limited feeling that the information within management budgets promoted cost awareness. However, the majority of the target of hospital doctors who were intended to be budget holders reported that:

- the information which they received was irrelevant;
- the concept of management budgets seemed inappropriate;
- they had no control over the costs assigned to them;
- there were not sufficient resources to make the new budgetary system work;
- there were no incentives or sanctions in the system;
- management showed a low commitment to the new system; and
- the information generated was inaccurate and the information provided was also difficult to use (Lapsley, 2001a).

In addition to these technical deficiencies, the hospital doctors were puzzled by the fact that there was no official evaluation of the trials. This tale of ineffectiveness is a story of poorly designed systems which do not connect with targeted, potential users. The subsequent reform – resource management – was envisaged as a more sophisticated variant of management budgeting which would generate reports which included both financial information and non-financial information on medical activity. This was targeted at clinicians with management responsibilities. This did not function, as intended. When the management consultants who are supporting one case study site completed their tasks, the system stopped operating. The IT system was so labour-intensive and time-consuming that more traditional systems of data collection were favoured at this study site. This second reform, resource management, was also a failure at both sites. However, a variant of the initial reform had taken hold at both sites, with some success as measured by the willingness of key actors to use and act upon this budgetary information. As one clinical director with budgetary responsibility at one of these case study sites said when expressing his contentment with the operation of his unit's budget:

> *We have monthly financial reports. There is a chap from the finance department who brings them down to a size you can understand. The report is basically the same, but he selects out information. He highlights the important things. You know who to go to, there is one person who knows how our directorate works.*

The previous statement casts the accountant in the role of interpreter. But, most importantly, these clinical directors are willing to listen and to act, as the following clinical director's comments explain:

> *In many ways being a clinical director with a budget is more productive and more satisfactory. I have a budget which I can manipulate and I am able to achieve much more .... . I have been able to make changes in running the wards and improving standards by the empowering process of having the budget and the related authority from that.*

The reasons for the success of these examples of budgets as change mechanisms were not just a question of kinds of information supplied, the manner of the support (with the accountant as interpreter) or the effectiveness of the technology. The manner and the timing of implementation of these budgets was critical, as was the idea of organisational memory/forgetfulness in which past failures were forgotten and new achievements went on to succeed. However, this successful implementation of clinical budgeting at these study sites needs to be placed into context. At best, this use of budgeting as a change mechanism is developmental, *ie* the successful introduction of a new management practice.

Case study experience: (2) Local Government

The experiences of the NHS were those of an organisation which did not have budgetary procedures for its key actors (hospital doctors), the kind of situation Wallander (*op. cit.*) advocates, and its struggle to implement budgets for hospital doctors, which, ultimately, did work. The situation of local government is different. It has well established budgetary mechanisms and here the issue is whether they have been instrumental in facilitating the government's change agenda, or not. A crucial element of the investigation of budgets within local government is the context of this part of the public sector. It is intensely political, and there are often significant differences between central and local government. The political dimension, with elected officials in charge, has resulted in the observation that key policy makers may adopt a short run perspective, given the prospect of periodic elections. Nevertheless, within this distinctive environment, the budget has been regarded as a dominant form of control. However, this control emphasis points to the ineffectiveness of the budget in local government as a lever for exerting policy change.

Within local government there has been an explicit change agenda within the modernisation policy of the New Labour government. A major dimension of this is the introduction of quality as an explicit objective of local government services. The Scottish government has also introduced the concept of Best Value (Scottish Office, 1997, 1998), which is extended to take the focus of improvement in local government services beyond cost savings to encourage cost: quality trade offs. While the major emphasis has been on quality, the government has recognised the significance of budgetary information and the need to shift this from being regarded as a control device to one for planning by the introduction of three-year budgeting for the first time.

The case study evidence was gathered from four local authorities (two cities and two rural authorities). In all of these local authorities significant changes were evident, many in response to the government's policy of modernisation. These included new organisational structures, with de-departmentalisation to encourage local authority services to have 'joined-up' or 'cross-cutting' services, which provide a holistic approach to local government services rather than a narrow departmental lens. An important part of this modernisation agenda has entailed a shift from inputs to outputs. In particular, there is now a focus on the concerns of citizens and users of services rather than having the traditional emphasis on the views of deliverers of services. These dimensions of the new public service were articulated by the introduction of three-year service plans and action plans.

In all of this, the impact of the budget as a change mechanism in local government retained its significance. The importance of financial constraints placed this centre stage in local government policy making. The persistent downward pressure on expenditure plans caused by government imposed efficiency gain targets (real terms reductions) in expenditure plans has reaffirmed the importance of the financial constraint. But this operates at a global level, as a brake on the overall activities of these councils. This 'braking function' is accentuated at the case study sites by the lack of significant investment to enhance IT facilities (see chapter five). Existing budgetary procedures were augmented by 'star chambers' at which all budget proposals were analysed carefully. In this restricted sense, the budget in local authorities can be described as a change mechanism.

However, the particular form of this change mechanism is important. Within the case studies, the moves to three-year financial budgets were tentative and there was not enough emphasis on the development of policy-led budgets. There was continued use of incremental budgeting in these councils. As one budget holder commented.

We are not doing policy led budgeting, we are just doing the old fashioned incremental budgeting. And I think it will be a long number of years before we are really making budgets a policy.

These comments were also accompanied by other reservations about the quality of accounting information (inaccuracies, lacking necessary detail, not user-friendly, although with modest steps in the direction of commitment-based accounting information) which undermines the role of accounting in effecting change. Much of this state of affairs can be attributed to a lack of investment and support for accounting functions which tend to suffer relative to front-line services in a situation of cutbacks and financial entrenchment. Ultimately, the role of budgeting in local government, in its present form, remains at the developmental state.

Conclusion

In this chapter, the researchers have noted the recent critique of budgeting which suggests that this accounting technique has outlived its usefulness as a change mechanism in modern organisations. This criticism of the budget is counter to the traditional views that the budget in public sector organisations is a major instrument of control and a lever for change.

Case study evidence from the NHS has been examined. This is an area of complexity. The budgeting practices of the NHS have often been criticised as incremental and insensitive to the needs for change. They have also been criticised as being partial, with major areas of expenditure within the clinical domain not being included in budgetary processes. The evidence reported here suggests that the trajectory of change for this kind of budgeting – of clinical budgeting - is rather long. The design and timing of the implementation are crucial to its success. The perception of failure is deeply rooted in the literature. This evidence presented here is counter to that prevailing view.

Also, the situation in local government has been examined. This is also an area of some complexity with a distinct political overlay to the workings of local government officials. There are distinct changes being introduced in local government where the budget has always been a dominant instrument for implementing local authority plans. However, the introduction of three-year budgeting within local government presents a significant departure from the practice of annuality which had the effect of distorting patterns of expenditure, especially at financial year ends. Overall, however, this study found that, while budgets retained their significance, this was more as a crude, binding constraint, rather than as a policy led financial instrument.

The evidence gathered as part of this study reaffirms the significance of the budget as a change mechanism in the public sector. It has given accounting information visibility in addressing policy priorities and the effective management of resources. However, it can, on occasion, be seen as a blunt instrument rather than a sensitive management tool. In terms of the three change states identified in chapter one, the budget has been classified as having a developmental role in changing the public sector.

CHAPTER FOUR

VALUE-FOR-MONEY AUDIT

Value for money (VFM) auditing was first introduced as a statutory requirement for local government in the UK with the creation of the Audit Commission for England and Wales in 1983 under the terms of the Local Government Finance Act of 1982. This gave auditors responsibility for investigating whether proper arrangements were in place to secure economy, efficiency and effectiveness in the use of local authority resources. The Audit Commission has responsibility for arranging the audit (which may mean its staff undertaking audits or sub-contracting to professional firms of accountants) of local government and related bodies and the operational branches of the National Health Service in England. In Scotland, the Accounts Commission discharges similar duties and has been charged with responsibility for VFM audits, since 1 April 1983, under the terms of the Local Government (Scotland) Act of 1983. Also, since 1 January 1984, the National Audit Office was established, under the terms of the National Audit of 1983, to undertake VFM audits of central government. With the advent of the Scottish Parliament, Audit Scotland now has an over-arching responsibility for such audits in public services in Scotland.

Value-for-money (VFM) is now a taken for granted technique for achieving changes in public services. It is now so well accepted that it is embedded in the language, policy statements, manuals and guidance of national audit offices and of professional accounting bodies and professional accounting firms. The search for VFM can be seen as the fundamental driving force for much of the changes which have been wrought in the public sector in recent decades. The importance of VFM has achieved a new significance in the context of the current UK government's modernisation policy.

VFM in modernisation

The present Labour government, which was elected in May 1997, introduced the Best Value concept in its election manifesto (Labour Party 1997). In its report to the Secretary of State for Scotland, the Best Value Taskforce developed guidance on the concept of Best Value and made the following observation:

> *The report recognises that significant elements of Best Value are already being developed by local government and the Accounts Commission. It seeks to build on established and emerging arrangements and processes. For example, it recognises that Scottish Councils already have a statutory duty to seek value for money in all their activities and that audit procedures exist to monitor their performance in this respect.* (Scottish Office, 1997, p.1)

The UK's Cabinet Office (1999) defined modernisation as having three elements: (1) ensuring that policy is more joined up and strategic; (2) making sure that public service users, not providers, are the focus, by matching services more closely to people's lives; and (3) delivering public services that are high quality and efficient. This explicit focus on modernisation is reinforced by subsequent policy documents which place VFM in the context of other policy changes.

One such initiative was the creation of a Best Value taskforce (Scottish Office, 1997, 1998). Within the detailed guidance on these elements of Best Value, there is reference to the need for performance monitoring and explicit reference to the need to achieve value for money in service provision. In operationalising the concept of Best Value, this taskforce made explicit the central role occupied by VFM:

> *Best Value is about continuous improvement, learning and applying best practice from other councils and other agencies to improve quality and value for money.* (Scottish Office, 1997, p.1).

This recognises that significant elements of Best Value are already being developed by Local Government and the Accounts Commission. It seeks to build on established and emerging arrangements and processes. For example, it recognises that Scottish Councils already have a statutory duty to seek value-for-money in all their activities and that audit procedures exist to monitor their performance in this respect.

VFM audit in practice

As noted above, the expression VFM is now embedded in everyday language and discussion about the performance of the public sector. However, as shall be seen in this study, although there have been attempts to define this expression, undertaking of VFM audits is problematic in practice. An attempt to describe the meaning of value for money can be found in the guidance offered to prospective professional accountants who intend to pursue a career in audit. It draws on the manner in which value for money is embedded in everyday language to explain the concept in relation to an advertising campaign for a household detergent, as follows:

> *Although much has been written about value for money, there is no great mystique about the concept. The term is common in everyday speech and so is the idea. To drive the point home, think of a bottle of Fairy Liquid. If we believe the advertising, Fairy is good 'value for money' because it washes half as many plates again as any other washing up liquid. Bottle for bottle, it may be more expensive, but plate for plate it is cheaper. Not only this but Fairy gets plates 'squeaky' clean. To summarise, Fairy gives us VFM because it exhibits the following characteristics:*
>
> *(a) Economy (more clean plates per pound)*
> *(b) Efficiency (more clean plates per squirt)*
> *(c) Effectiveness (plates as clean as they should be)*

(ACCA, 1993, pp.438-439)

In 1990, the Consultative Committee of Accountancy Bodies (cited in Pickwell, 1990) issued an audit brief on value for money audit and this defines the terms economy, efficiency and effectiveness as follows:

(a) Economy: obtaining the appropriate quantity and quality of physical, human and financial resources (inputs) at lowest cost. An activity would not be economic, if, for example, there was over-staffing or failure to purchase materials of requisite quality at the lowest available price.

(b) Efficiency: this is the relationship between goods or services produced (outputs) and the resources used to produce them. An efficient operation produces the maximum output for any given set of resource inputs: or it has minimum inputs for any given quantity and quality of product or service provided.

(c) Effectiveness: this is concerned with how well an activity is achieving its policy objectives or other intended effects.

In this part of this paper the study draws on evidence obtained from an expert group of VFM auditors all of whom have considerable experience of public sector audit. The exchanges with these auditors resulted in an analysis of four key dimensions of VFM: (1) the response of professional groups to VFM studies; (2) the usefulness of VFM; (3) practical issues in the implementation of VFM; and (4) the future of VFM.

On (1), there is a general view in the public sector that professional groups are seen as powerful barriers to change. However, this study provided a more complex story. It had three sets of responses: (a) members of public services organisations (regardless of professional groups) are generally positive to VFM, even though possibly hostile, initially; (b) some professional groups have the main preoccupation of how they will be affected by any VFM study; and (c) finance professionals tend to react most positively to VFM audits compared to other professional groups. These findings suggest VFM continues to have the potential to be a change mechanism.

In terms of the utility of VFM audit, these practitioners saw a major general benefit from focussing on 'Best Practice'. In terms of specific benefits, they cited (a) operational benefits: (improving management systems and processes, identification and discontinuation of redundant jobs, assisting in property risk management, sharpening up of management thinking), and (b) strategic benefits: (investments linked to performance and resource allocation, and articulation of corporate planning, service planning and budgetary control). They also pointed to the 'policing' role of VFM: ensuring resources are utilised in the most effective manner.

While the previous statements about the utility of VFM underpin the importance of this mechanism for changing public services, there are other issues raised by our expert group which cast doubt on this interpretation of the significance of VFM. In particular, these experienced VFM auditors had all encountered serious challenges or difficulties in the conduct of VFM audits which undermine the idea of VFM as taken for granted or embedded in audit practice. In terms of practical challenges, these auditors identified the difficulties of getting comparable information, lack of computerised management systems (see chapter 5), difficulties of disentangling the interdependencies of service provision, forming opinions on qualitative measures, and dealing with non 'textbook situations'.

They also had reservations over the quality of evidence as certain indicators were highly subjective, and there were conflicts of interpretation. These auditors had also encountered assessment issues: local interpretations of statutory guidance; disputes between departments; and human resource issues. Quality issues were a difficulty, particularly the ambiguity of quality, links between quality and VFM, and a lack of robust measures of quality. All this raises questions about the sustainability of VFM as a change mechanism.

VFM audit: The future

This expert group was asked about the future of VFM in securing change in the public sector. Within the group there were expressions of need for the improvement of the institutional setting of VFM audit (for instance, greater transferability of practices across sectors and greater cohesion amongst oversight bodies). Overall, this expert group saw a greater need for VFM audits and saw this as crucial for the new development of 'Best Value'. However, there were misgivings, too. There was potential for Best Value to marginalise VFM studies, as the VFM contribution may only be short term. This group also saw the potential for Best Value to become a 'straitjacket'. There was also a real danger of displacement of resources from front line service provision to the demonstration that resources were being used effectively. The group also stressed that VFM studies were not replica studies, but were often unique. In the current climate, this raises questions about the continued role of VFM as a change mechanism; although its past contributions cannot be challenged.

Conclusion

In the study, some problem areas in VFM audit have been identified relating to (i) practical execution of VFM, (ii) the quality of evidence available to them, (iii) assessment issues and, in particular, (iv) the problematic nature of 'quality'. The practical problem areas in VFM audit are perhaps best illuminated when one interviewee summarised VFM audit as follows:

> There is no magic word. Instinct, gut feeling or rumours may direct you to particular studies, but you have no real knowledge until you have carried out studies, recorded and analysed the results.

This demonstrates that VFM, as a practice, cannot be taken for granted. It is not necessarily about mimicry. There may be significant challenges to VFM auditors in the conduct of studies, in the shaping of the audit approach and the interpretation of results.

However, there is sustained evidence in the literature which supports the view that VFM audits have been a key mechanism in achieving substantive change in the public sector in the past two decades. For this reason, we see VFM audit as fitting within the sphere of transitional change which recognises the contribution of VFM to the reorganisation of public sector entities. Nonetheless there are question marks over its continued role with the arrival of Best Value. There are also difficulties of addressing the more difficult and contentious issues of efficiency and effectiveness. In a sense, the easier VFM exercises have been conducted in the earlier years of its life. Now the challenges are greater. Indeed, in the following chapters, this study identifies two major areas where there would be considerable merit in high level VFM studies: (1) the effectiveness of major IT initiatives across the public sector and (2) the use of management consultants in effecting change in the public sector.

CHAPTER FIVE

INFORMATION TECHNOLOGY INITIATIVES

There has been considerable stress placed on information technology initiatives to transform the public sector. Reference has been made in the discussion of budgeting in public sector organisations (see chapter 3) to the manner in which the state of IT has been a constraint in the development of effective systems within these organisations. However, despite such 'micro' level difficulties, there have been large scale, grand visionary designs on the use of IT as a change mechanism which would transform the public sector. This policy option is longstanding within the UK, but it has seen fresh impetus with the modernisation strategy of the Labour administrations of 1997 and 2001. This is made explicit in the following policy statement (Cabinet Office, 1999):

> *We will use new technology to meet the needs of citizens and business, and not trail behind technological developments. We will: develop an IT strategy for Government which will establish cross-government co-ordination machinery and frameworks on such issues as use of digital signatures, and smart cards, websites and call centres; benchmark progress against targets for electronic services.*

The development of non-trivial IT systems in the UK public sector is usually undertaken by outside contractors and consultants. This is a consequence of the long-term governmental policy of outsourcing IT service and development requirements in order to improve value for money. This policy has not been without its flaws. The UK public sector, with certain specific exceptions, has outsourced so much of its in-house IT expertise that it is now effectively a naïve client when acquiring IT services and perhaps even more importantly there exists the prospect that the advice the Civil Service provides to ministers on all policy matters may be of less than its usual quality when it comes to matters of IT related policy.

Irrespective of the method of procuring IT services, this reliance on the use of IT has not been without difficulties. Indeed, it has been estimated that, out of an annual UK expenditure of *c.* £7-£8 billion the failure rate of public sector IT development projects may be in excess of 50% (Brown, 2001). There have been numerous high profile cases of information technology failures (essentially systems which do not work), which are wide in scope, across the public sector. The following are a few examples:

Wessex Regional Health Authority Regional Information Systems Plan (RISP):

The case of an ambitious information system being planned and developed without any effective management controls being exercised over the contractors and consultants involved.

The Immigration and Nationality Directorate Casework Programme:

The system development specification was for a computerised copy of the existing manual asylum application processing system. However at the same time, and completely unconnected with the computerisation project, the Directorate was also running a business process re-engineering exercise to streamline the manual system.

The Benefits Agency and Post Office Counters Ltd, Benefit Payment Card project (Pathway)

A massive, over ambitious, integrated fraud avoidance/automated banking system built for two purchasers each with different objectives and requirements.

The Benefits Agency National Insurance Recording System (NIRS2)

NIRS2 is the replacement information system for the original National Insurance Recording System (NIRS1). NIRS2 became necessary to deal with changes in the legislation regarding pension provisions and was timetabled to be operational from April 1997. The initial decision that a NIRS1 replacement was required was taken in 1992. The Agency first attempted to undertake the project itself but failed to make any headway. Only in 1994 did it decide to put the project out to tender using the Public Finance Initiative (PFI) as a means of financing the project. The tendering process was completed in May 1995 when a contract was signed with Andersen Consulting. (The general issue of the impact of management consultants in effecting change in the public sector is taken up in the next chapter). This left 22 months for the contractor to develop what is one of the largest information systems in the UK. Despite this being a contracted PFI project, which is supposed to ensure that the project risks are transferred from the purchaser to the contractor, the contractor has been allowed to re-negotiate both the cost and the delivery timetable and even by the end of 2002 the NIRS2 system was not fully functional. The Agency was criticised not only for poor management of deadlines but also for having no contingency plans should its initial deadline not be met.

IT initiatives as change mechanisms

The issue was examined by scrutinising published reports in the public domain. Two particularly valuable sources of information are the reports of the Committee of Public Accounts (CPA) and those of the National Audit Office (NAO), both organisations which have been extremely critical of the handling of major IT developments within the public sector. The CPA published a major report summarising the issues identified in 25 NAO reports highlighting serious problems in IT development, project management and procurement (CPA, 2000).

In other words, IT initiatives had failed to be effective change mechanisms.

The CPA made a series of recommendations about the lessons to be learned from these repeated development, management and procurement failures. These include the observation that key decisions about IT systems are business decisions not technical ones, that the commitment of senior management is essential; and identifying the end users and their needs is critical to the success of a project. They also noted that scale and complexity can easily lead to failure, and advocated breaking projects down into manageable sub-components. Further, they commented that the management and oversight of a project by skilled and knowledgeable managers is essential. In particular, project managers have to be imaginative and skilled in risk control as well as in project management, and a high degree of professionalism is required in the definition, negotiation and management of IT contracts. Furthermore, they observed that contingency plans must be in place and must provide adequate service levels. Finally, they recommended a post-implementation review of the project as essential for both monitoring the success of the project and for learning from it.

The Cabinet Office (2000) responded by broadly accepting the criticisms made by the CPA and making its own set of recommendations. This 2000 report sought to address the CPA criticisms by improving the focus on business change across Government and outlining methods for achieving and maintaining this. It made a number of recommendations to encourage good leadership and to establish clear lines of responsibility for IT-based change programmes and projects and to improve project management across Government, with particular emphasis on the management of risk. The report also advocated modular and incremental approaches to implementing IT-related change to improve the measurement and realisation of benefits. It further recommended taking a more strategic approach to suppliers, addressing problems with current guidance and setting out the actions suppliers need to take. The Cabinet Office was also concerned to stress the need to provide the in-house skills needed to deliver improvements in the handling of

IT-related change including a system of peer review and requirements and mechanisms for obtaining and sharing good practice. The Cabinet Office has turned the matter of implementing this guidance over to the recently established Office of Government Commerce (OGC) which has done a highly creditable job of expanding and promulgating the Cabinet Office's recommendations and in integrating this material with its more general procurement guidance.

While the recommendations of both the CPA and the Cabinet Office are sensible it must be pointed out that by nature they represent very basic, unexceptional and largely self-evident advice on contract and project management. What is surprising is that such basic recommendations have to be made at all. Their very existence constitutes an acknowledgment of systemic failure in this area and does little to encourage faith in the management of a public sector which, by necessity, purchases a significant level of expertise from the private sector.

In addition to the Cabinet Office response, the Computer Services and Software Association (CSSA) (the main industry association representing UK private sector suppliers of IT services), carried out a survey of its members for their views on improving the provision of IT services to the public sector. The CSSA agrees with the Cabinet Office that there are significant problems in the management of projects by the public sector, but it also recognises that there are supply side problems and notes that:

> *IT suppliers have on occasion been over-optimistic in planning major programmes and may have set false expectations. The industry should avoid these practices.*

Brown (2001) has undertaken a further analysis and has concluded that among the major issues are the lack of suitable management capacity in the public sector, weak procurement mechanisms, including the relatively small number of contractors who are capable of taking on large public sector projects, and the inherent complexity of software development itself.

Despite these issues, the reliance on IT initiatives to transform the public sector remains an important strand of the government's policy to modernise the public sector. But, on the basis of this evidence, there must be significant doubt about the effectiveness of IT initiatives as a change mechanism for the UK public sector. At best, we can classify the contribution of IT initiatives as developmental, after Costello (1994). They have fallen far short of the transition and of the intended aim of transformation.

Conclusion

The problem of IT development failure in the public sector is complex and it is unlikely to yield to simple measures. The contract and project management guidance currently being produced by the OGC is an excellent first step, but much more than that is required. The public sector must make every effort to lose its 'naïve client' status, requiring that significant educational efforts are made. These should start at the top with senior policy makers, as it is they who ultimately bear responsibility as the direct or indirect initiators of many of the larger failed IT projects. At the policy advisory and implementation levels education is certainly required but a culture change is also necessary. Managers in what is a largely risk averse public sector, have to learn that there is more to risk management than simply passing responsibility down the management chain. This may entail changing the way that some public sector workers are managed and rewarded and it may also mean bringing in people with experience of good business practice from the private sector to function either in an executive or mentoring role.

The procurement process presents some serious actual and potential problems. A close reading of the relevant NAO and CPA reports on IT project failures demonstrates that reliance on the tendering process informed by the calculation of a public sector comparator does little to ensure that value for money is received from suppliers. Equally apparent is that PFI financing does not always meet its objective of isolating the public sector from additional costs associated with IT project development risk.

A potential procurement problem is inherent in the small number of IT service suppliers who are equipped to handle large public sector projects. Such a restricted marketplace is unlikely to provide the most efficient market. This is compounded by the naïve client problem ensuring that these same suppliers are called upon to provide the public sector with consultancy services (see also chapter 6) including the provision of advice and sometimes even the provision of information for calculating public sector comparators as a prelude to tendering. Pursuing this policy might well be effective in the short term, but is likely to establish the major suppliers and ensure that there is little effective competition for them so becoming counter-productive in the medium to long term as well as being out of step with European competition policy.

The much-vaunted reliance of government policy on using IT as a mechanism for transforming the public sector does not appear warranted on the basis of the evidence presented in this chapter. There have been serial failures of extremely expensive, over-ambitious IT projects which were intended to make substantive change to the management of public services. The government has now realised that this is an issue, but its response confirms the likely longevity of this problem.

management consultants on their perceptions of the impact of their work in the public sector in which the study seeks to determine the effectiveness of management consultants as change agents. In this study the views of management consultants was obtained from both the large, established consultancy firms and from the small consultancies.

Impact of management consultants

The starting point in discovering whether management consultants were indeed the powerful change agents depicted in the literature was to explore the kind of work management consultants did. This gave interesting results. The literature depicts management consultants as significant change agents, but the reality is that, for many of the consultants interviewed, public sector assignments were more mundane. A variety of tasks identified as being undertaken by management consultants in the public sector included the following:

1. an extra resource (as a substitute for internal staff)
2. to work on a particular problem
3. to introduce a new technique
4. as a 'political' appointment to resolve internal disputes

The first item, which is increasingly used, is a response by public sector organisations to reductions in establishment level, after successive years of budget reductions. This employment of management consultants can be seen as a casualisation of the labour force of public sector organisations. The second and third items fit with the more popular image of what management consultants are appointed to do. The final category fits the situation where the organisation is not seeking a task-specific solution and the management consultant's report is seen more in terms of legitimising the organisation's activities. One of the management consultants interviewed expressed this phenomenon in the following terms:

One of the easiest ways for an organisation to waste money is to use a consultant and not do anything about what they say. And there are occasions when that happens, not much happens as a result of the work we do, and I can think of one organisation where they actually wanted the job doing more as a political requirement within their organisation, to satisfy honour on all sides.

None of the above uses of management consultants could be seen as significant enough in themselves to merit the accolade of the management consultant as a significant 'change agent'. Much of the above work places the work of management consultants in the developmental state, or potentially in the transitional state (after Costello, 1994).

Indeed, in discussions with the management consultants, there was no indication that any of those interviewed felt that they had a mission to change organisations. The motivation of the management consultants interviewed in this study was more that of professionals who had a set of skills, an expertise which they had used to secure well remunerated employment. Most of the management consultants interviewed described themselves as bringing an expert, outside view – an injection of fresh thinking. Given this perspective, that management consultants see themselves as delivering professional expertise rather than transforming the public sector into a 'New Public Sector' with a new vision, we should not be surprised if our classification of their impact as a change mechanism remains at the developmental or transitional state (after Costello, *op. cit.*). This is taken up further, below.

The changing public sector

Next the management consultant's perceptions of the public sector were explored. Specifically, the researchers sought to determine if, in their view, the public sector had been transformed and, if so, what was their role in this transformation. A major observation by all of these management consultants was that one continuing distinguishing characteristic of the public sector was the slowness of decision making. However, these management consultants had noticed an improvement in the working practices of recent years, particularly with attempts at increased flexibility. However, as the following comment by one management consultant illustrates, this has to be taken in the context of the low starting point for public sector organisations:

> *Yes, there is much more flexibility and less standardisation. But this is from a low base in the early '80s. Still much more needs to be done … .*

They did comment, though, that some public sector organisations were still bureaucratic and resistant to change and there was still a 'tendency' to more standardisation in these organisations.

In the view of these management consultants, the accounting function of the UK public sector has improved, with greater visibility. A major facet of this visibility was attributed to the presence of more qualified accountants in the public sector. However, in their view, there were still sections of the public sector (notably central government) where the status of accountants could be higher. The numbers, mix and qualifications of accountants in the public sector are differentiated sharply from the private sector, which has a considerably stronger accounting presence. Overall, there was no strong, unanimous view amongst these management consultants that the importance of accounting had improved significantly in the public sector. They also considered that public sector management was stronger than previously and that the quality of public sector management is better. However, they identified a number of limitations on this, including the relatively low pay of public sector managers, and the political constraints on decision making. Furthermore, these consultants identified the power of professional groups as a major constraint in decision making. In conclusion, their view was that public sector management was stronger but only in certain parts of the public sector.

These comments are indicative of some changes but one dimension of whether 'transformation' of the public sector has been achieved or not is the extent to which the public sector adopts private sector ideas. In the view of these management consultants, the public sector was generally more business-like, but there still remained a distinct, public sector ethos. They had encountered what they described as 'mimicry', without any clear understanding of why private sector ideas should be adopted. They also made the observation that there are considerable variations across the sub-sectors (health, local and central government, other not-for-profit institutions) of the public sector. To achieve a greater convergence with the private sector these management consultants observed that public sector organisations had to (1) develop closer links to their customers and (2) change their cultures. These findings are supportive of public sector changes, but not of transformation.

Conclusion

These findings are not indicative of management consultants as powerful change agents in the public sector. Furthermore, on assessing the impact of these management consultants, the major frustration of consultancy in the public sector was that often their reports were not acted upon. The visibility of the management consultancy profession is not in doubt, but these findings suggest that a common view, namely that they are dominant in the transformation of the public sector, has to be regarded with some scepticism. In terms of the Costello framework the contribution of management consultants in effecting change is developmental and at best transitional.

This evidence suggests that there is a need for:

1. a more careful evaluation of the use of management consultants by public sector organisations;

2. the development of central policies (eg by central government or oversight agencies) on the effective use of management consultancy services; and

3. further research into (a) the effectiveness of, and the implementation of reports by management consultants and (b) the use of management consultants as a substitute for staff shed from establishment figures for reasons of economy or efficiency gains. This latter aspect of management consultancy services could reduce or even negate declared efficiency gains by public sector institutions by masking that substantially the same, or greater, costs of service provision were being incurred.

CHAPTER SEVEN

THE ACCOUNTANT IN THE 'NEW PUBLIC SECTOR' - COMPETENCIES AND SKILLS

The intended transformation of the UK public sector has the potential for major implications for the everyday working lives of public sector accountants (Lapsley and Oldfield, 2000). While the previous chapters of this report have pointed to new understandings of the actual and potential significance of accounting and accountants (as, for example, management consultants) and of accounting mechanisms (such as budgets, VFM studies and computerised information systems) in achieving a transformation of the UK's public sector, there remains little doubt about the visibility of, and importance of accounting in the 'New Public Sector'. Nevertheless, there remains an important agenda to determine the effects of such changes on accountants. This matter is addressed within this chapter.

Pressures on accountants

Public sector accountants continue to face pressures to identify efficiency gains and to demonstrate value-for-money in services. This pressure is in the context of significant changes involving the restructuring of public sector organisations and the introduction of new styles of management to replace the old-style public administration. These changes must also be seen in the context of wider societal expectations of the UK public sector in particular, expectations of cultural change, with the citizen now regarded as a 'consumer'. All of this is happening in a situation where there is a strong emphasis on public-private partnerships.

The Public Sector Accountant of the future

As part of this programme of research, the researchers sought the views of an expert group of senior accountants, eminent members of the UK accounting profession in the public sector, with significant experience of major changes in their own industries or organisations and with significant members of finance personnel within their organisations, on how the accountant of the future would be affected by all these changes (Lapsley and Oldfield, 2001(a)).

In this part of the research programme, five major dimensions of the role of the public sector accountant of the future were identified. This entailed both continuity and change: the potential for continuing existing practice as well as developing and evolving new practices. The five dimensions identified were as follows:

1. *Regularity*: establishing the main budget, overseeing preparation of the accounts
2. *Inward looking*: greater focus on management accounting for best use of resources
3. *Strategic Accounting*: a greater pre-occupation with the position of the organisation *vis-à-vis* other organisations
4. *Liaison*: IT advances of devolved management structures, shifting the focus of Chief Financial officer to a central liaison or co-ordinating role?
5. *Entrepreneurial*: a major emphasis on income generation and on radical reappraisal of services, with a sensitivity to market opportunities.

Competencies and skills

When these dimensions were discussed with the expert group, a pattern was revealed which suggested significant shifts in the practices of UK public sector accountants. In summary:

- regularity was a major consideration in the past and at present, but would be of lessening importance in the future.
- the 'inward-looking' role was of major importance now and in the past, less so in the future.

Given the demise of 'regularity' and the 'inward-looking' functions, it was interesting to see the expert group's view of the future:

- strategic accounting was regarded as being of limited importance now, whereas it was expected to be a dominant activity in the future;
- liaison was regarded as a slight role now: with the prospect of a significant increase in the future; and
- the entrepreneurial role is one in which it was thought public sector accounting had a slight involvement in the past and the present, but in which it would have a major role in the future.

In addition, the competencies of the accountant of the future were discussed with this expert group. A summary of their views is shown in table 7.1. This shows a significant shift from public sector accounting as it is currently practised to a kind of 'public sector financial manager'. The views of this group on the increasing importance of marketing, human resource and general management skills raises issues not only for existing professionals in the field, but also for the recruitment and training of would be accountants in the 'New Public Sector'.

Table 7.1:   The Competencies of Public Sector and Not-for-Profit Accountants

Competencies	Now	Future
• **Communication skills**	Essential	Essential
• **Quantification**	Core	Still important
• **Financial expertise**	Central	Central
• **Marketing skills**	Little evidence	Increasingly important (income generation)
• **Human resource skills**	Limited	Limited, slow to realise importance
• **General management skills**	Limited	Increasingly very important
• **Other**	Political skills	IT skills an absolute necessity

Accounting practices

This expert group was also asked about the importance of specific accounting practices. Surprisingly the shift to accrual accounting, which is manifest in local government (with capital accounting), the health service (with capital charging), in the charity sector (with depreciation accounting) and in central government (with the introduction of resource accounting) was taken for granted. The debate about whether the public sector should or should not have capital asset accounting and full accrual accounting is over. It is everywhere throughout the public and not-for-profit sector of the economy. In terms of techniques and practice, this expert group had two interesting observations to make regarding the skills and competencies of the public sector accountant of the future:

1. management techniques (specifically strategic management accounting – especially benchmarking – and the Balanced Scorecard) were where the future lay, and
2. 'softer' management skills would be more important than any specific techniques.

In conclusion, one member made the following observation on the significance of the adoption of accrual accounting:

If we take resource accounting, the initial feel was that this was about tracking debtors and creditors. Then we went on to realise that it was about capturing assets as well. And now suddenly we realise that this is not about accounting, but it is about culture and managing the business rather than keeping the score.

This is a fascinating statement about the subtleties of the impacts of accounting in the transformation process within the public sector. The move from cash-based and modified accrual to full accrual accounting within the public sector can be seen as a dramatic change, as a move towards closer convergence with the practices of the private sector. However, as the above comment by a leading member of the accounting profession illustrates, it is not the change in accounting practice which is of greatest significance. The transformation process is much more about wider issues, about the softer skills discussed above in bringing about changes in corporate culture.

Conclusion

The findings of this research, based on interviews with members of an expert group of leading accountants in the public sector, pointed to changing circumstances for the public sector accountant of the present and of the future. The traditional importance of the regularity function of accounting was likely to decline. Similarly the inward-looking focus on the management of best use of resources within the organisation was likely to decline.

For the public sector accountant of the future, the role was seen as entrepreneurial, strategic and with a more significant liaison role than in the past. In terms of competencies, it was considered that traditional skills of communication, financial expertise and quantification would remain important. However, it was envisaged that increasingly the public sector accountant of the future would be required to have skills in marketing, human resources and general management.

These findings have major implications for employers of public sector accountants in terms of the skills mix required of employees in the future. These findings also have important implications for professional accounting bodies. They raise issues of both necessary competencies as part of formal training and as part of post-qualifying training.

All of the above findings point to a continued turbulence for the public sector in the UK. However, this is an arena where there will continue to be a demand for accounting. This research suggests, though, that the public sector accountant of the future in the UK will be significantly different from his modern day equivalent. Changing circumstances, changing accounting and accountants, as the 'New Public Sector' becomes embedded in the economy.

CHAPTER EIGHT

DIFFUSION OF NEW ACCOUNTING TECHNIQUES IN THE PUBLIC SECTOR

Introduction

The findings of the previous chapter suggest that public sector accountants are now placing, or will in the future place less emphasis on accounting technique. The picture presented in the previous chapter is that of a supplementing of technique by the softer skills of entrepreneurship, general management and marketing. To examine this further, a survey was conducted of the practices of accountants within the public sector. This survey was intended to extend the views of the expert group as discussed in chapter seven, to determine the impact of changes in technique on accounting practices. *Prima facie*, it might be expected that the expected shift to softer skills and less emphasis on techniques and practices would be revealed by limited adoption of new techniques and practices. In this chapter the researchers report and comment upon findings from a questionnaire based study on the diffusion of accounting techniques and practices across three public sector areas: Health Care Trusts, Local Authority Organisations and Government Agencies.

Method and data

The survey investigates the everyday reality of management accounting techniques and practices in use in public sector organisations. To try and get the necessary breadth of data a survey across three areas of the public sector was conducted: the healthcare sector, local authorities and government agencies. This latter category of public sector organisations includes enterprise bodies, defence organisations, regulatory authorities and the Scottish Executive.

To obtain the necessary information on technical accounting practices, a survey was undertaken. The data collection method used was a postal survey of ICAS members, which included both structured and open questions about the accounting techniques and practices which are being used and the factors behind their adoption. The survey targeted 258 professionally qualified financial managers working in the public sector and 83 responses were received. When contacted, 85 members of this group indicated that they no longer had financial management responsibilities. This gave an effective response rate of 48%. A copy of the questionnaire is included at Appendix 2. The response was fairly even across all three areas although it was slightly higher from local authorities.

The first part of the questionnaire, intended to survey the techniques in use, was divided into three main categories: budgeting techniques; costing techniques; and performance measurement techniques. Each of these three categories was further divided into techniques that could potentially be used by these organisations. For instance the budgeting techniques listed included zero based budgeting, resource management, and activity based management; the costing techniques included target costing, activity based costing and strategic cost management; while performance measurement techniques included functional analysis, key performance indicators and the balanced scorecard (see glossary). The rest of the questionnaire consisted of open questions on the reasons for using certain techniques, the systems in place for monitoring the effectiveness of techniques and the contribution made by non-financial managers in the development of techniques.

Survey results

The survey results are shown in Table 8.1. The most widely used accounting technique reported by local authorities has been Key Performance Indicators (KPIs). KPIs were implemented on a voluntary basis when first developed but are now mandatory. Most improvements within local authority accounting appear to be stimulated by government legislation or exhortation. For example the introduction of Best Value Reviews and Continuous Improvement regimes were an important trigger for the implementation of KPIs within local authorities. As a result of these regimes the need for more cost/volume analysis of activities as applied to services arose and KPIs have been introduced mainly as a consequence of requests from oversight bodies for particular areas of information. KPIs are used on a continual basis although a few indicators are reported as not being relevant to the organisation and some test the timeliness of service rather than the real issue of quality of service.

Other contributing factors to the increased usage of KPIs have been the need to increase control over estimated levels of expenditure and the need to provide more information on how the money is being spent. Local authorities are also under pressure to improve both the budgetary process and the flow of information to the public and other interested parties.

Table 8.1: Most common accounting techniques in use

Accounting Technique	LA[1]	GA[2]	HC[3]	Percentage of Total Respondents
Budgeting Techniques				
Zero based budgeting	28%	9%	63%	33%
Resource management	14%	41%	100%	46%
Activity based management	25%	36%	38%	32%
Costing Techniques				
Target costing	3%	0%	8%	4%
Activity based costing	33%	14%	33%	28%
Strategic cost management	3%	4%	25%	10%
Performance Measurement				
Functional analysis	8%	0%	29%	12%
Key Performance Indicators	100%	82%	83%	90%
Balanced Scorecard	19%	14%	4%	13%

[1] Local authorities
[2] Government agencies
[3] Health care

Activity Based Costing (ABC) has also been introduced as part of the Best Value Review but is used to a lesser extent than KPIs. ABC was intended to aid management decisions after the government suspended Compulsory Competitive Tendering (CCT) and introduced Best Value for services. ABC was specifically recommended by the government task force as a key management tool in the review of the efficiency and effectiveness of services provided. ABC is intended to provide more refined estimates of costs than traditional allocation methods. Activity Based Management (ABM) was reported as being successful in areas such as building operations in winning contracts. ABC although in its early stages is reported as being useful in the best value framework.

Zero Based Budgeting (ZBB) was reported as being used as a result of the inaccuracy of the budgets evaluated at the reorganisation of local government in 1994. However, it only applies to a few areas, particularly direct labour organisations and has only been implemented to suit a specific purpose. This is because the actual outcomes varied considerably from the original budgets. Over the last four years local authorities have been required to achieve savings to reduce budgets to government guidelines. This is becoming increasingly more difficult and some of the respondents feel the need for ZBB to be expanded to cover more services in the future. ZBB is also favoured as its benefits can be seen and it provides more clarity in management information. However, in general, the respondents considered ZBB to be too time consuming and overly cumbersome to warrant widespread usage within the organisation. Resource Management was also indicated as being in use as a result of over spending of budgets and also to target switches in resources in specific services, eg away from residential care and into domiciliary care.

Respondents from the government agencies group reported that many of the accounting techniques employed in this area were determined centrally and are used on a network wide basis according to strategic directives and policy from the Scottish Executive. Accounting techniques in use within this group were introduced to aid decision making in growing organisations and as a result of re-organisation and local government legislation. The accounting techniques in use have evolved over time in response to a comprehensive spending review budget process used by the Scottish Executive and as a means of demonstrating value for money. The Government White Paper *Better Accounting for Taxpayers Money* (HM Government, 1995) has also been an important trigger in the adoption of new accounting techniques. The change in some organisations' status, revisions to the management structure, devolved responsibility and internal initiatives are other contributing factors. Changes in accounting techniques have also arisen from the need to produce efficiency measures.

Resource accounting and budgeting was introduced into central government in the UK in several phases to try and imitate the constraints of business within the public sector and to try to estimate a more precise cost of providing public services each year than is provided by cash expenditure. Other changes in accounting techniques in use have arisen in response to the need to account on an accruals basis for grant scheme liabilities at the end of each financial year, which was previously done on a simple cash basis.

The most successful reported accounting technique is KPI. In some cases KPIs were adopted as there had been a shift in the level and type of data used in the day-to-day management of the organisation. Other techniques reported as being relatively successful were ABC, Resource Management, incremental budgeting and variance monitoring. Resource accounting and budgeting is replacing cash accounting, which has always been used in this area. It is thought that this will fundamentally change the way departments within government agencies are managed by focusing more precisely on total resources held and consumed.

The changing environment of health care trusts has triggered the creation of new financial and management accounting systems within the finance sector of the NHS. Many of the changes that have occurred within the NHS financial system have resulted from the continual pressure from government on the NHS to reduce costs and to utilise limited resources more efficiently. NHS Trusts are also coming under pressure to provide information about, and justification of, resource allocation within the NHS system. NHS Trusts are now required to provide detailed costing of procedures, speciality costs and functional costs to external bodies and are expected to produce a

3% cost efficiency each year. The need to produce these cost efficiencies each year has driven the adoption of more advanced budgeting and costing techniques in some areas. The focus on cost pressures has also led to the adoption of performance indicators to allow comparison of performance between different NHS organisations performing similar tasks and for monitoring of new business cases and review of financial and operational performance.

Changes to previous budgeting techniques such as ZBB arose from the need to identify future cost pressures that may emerge during any year and for future years. In some cases a historical approach is used to identify the nature of, and recovery options from, previous financial problems and are adapted where appropriate to aid identification and resolution of current financial problems. Many of the changes in budgeting techniques employed by the NHS Trusts have been driven mainly by external factors – central government imperatives on the reporting of costs at different levels and costing efficiencies to be achieved.

Government policies have a major influence on which costing and budgeting techniques are employed. In most cases the most practical or effective technique to deal with the task in hand either for costing or budgeting an area or service is used. Some of the techniques in use within the NHS were introduced to make it more efficient, for example Resource Management techniques. For client based groups within hospitals, there are instances of Target Costing being introduced when the support services within hospitals had to compete with external suppliers for competitive tendering contracts.

Some NHS Trusts had a form of costing similar to ABC to cost services for the internal market, which supported their typical practices of recording cost by area or service. Both ABC and ZBB have limited support from respondents as the most straightforward and effective approach to controlling costs and making managers responsible for cost control. In most cases, incremental budgeting that rolls forward on an annual basis, appears to be the favoured method of budget construction.

KPIs were reported as being the most successful control mechanism both for Board level reporting and in reporting to the internal divisions of NHS organisations. KPIs have also been used to support performance review processes with local Trusts and have established trends and relationships between costs and other non-financial indicators. KPIs and strategic cost management were reported as having been used in conjunction with benchmarking. Other practices also include accountants' acting as business advisers to managers and budget holders to identify business cases and possible savings.

ZBB, Target Costing and ABM were reported as being used in some Trusts. Depending on the size of the task, rolling forward budgets and functional analysis are also used. Although recognition is given that other costing and budgeting techniques have their uses, functional analysis was indicated as performing the basis for ensuring financial targets were met. KPIs and functional analysis are considered equally successful in some areas. However, some participants feel that strategic cost management probably meets government policy objectives best, whilst others indicated a preference for ZBB. The general response, overall, is that NHS Trusts are becoming more and more controlled financially by Health Boards with additional resources being allocated through a bidding process and that different costing and budgeting techniques seem to be a side issue.

Overview

Firstly, it is abundantly clear that a wide array of accounting techniques are in use in the public sector, but it is notable that most of the activity is taking place in the area of performance measurement with nearly all public sector organisations reporting the use of one or more of the techniques listed in this survey. Notably, KPIs are used by a very high percentage of all public sector organisations with 100% of local authorities, 75% of government agencies and 83% of healthcare organisations reporting use of them. Other performance measurement techniques are less well used with the exception of 19%

of local authorities reporting use of the balanced scorecard and 29% of healthcare organisations using functional analysis. However, only KPIs are in use by most organisations in all three sectors in this survey. In terms of the perceived usefulness of the accounting techniques all the techniques in use received support from some individuals, but only KPIs seemed to create real enthusiasm amongst their users.

However, the second-largest grouping occurs in the budgeting techniques with Resource Management carrying a particularly high score. However, it should be noted that it was the area of healthcare which most influenced this statistic, with all healthcare organisations indicating that they used Resource Management as well as having used ZBB and possibly ABM. The reported use of these techniques in local authorities and government agencies is clearly much lower with a considerable percentage of these organisations not using any of these techniques.

Interestingly it is the area of costing which showed the least indication of innovations in practices with ABC being the only method that has any significant use across the public sector and even this is uneven. Strategic cost management is confined in its reported use to some 25% of healthcare organisations included in the study, but Target Costing has a very low showing across the board.

Conclusion

Judging from the data it would seem that the most important reasons for accounting innovation in public sector organisations are statute, regulation or other external pressure. While this does not preclude the possibility of internal innovation and experimentation with accounting techniques it overwhelms all other reasons. A strong example of this occurred in the setting of healthcare with the creation of the internal market in the NHS. All of the respondents indicated that the use of Resource Management arose in conjunction with this development. Also, many costing techniques in use have been required as a result of the CCT process. In the words of one respondent:

Many accounting techniques have been driven by the external need to report costs at different levels. Detailed costing of procedures, especially costs and functional costs are all externally required. The need to produce a 3% cost efficiency each year has driven the more advanced techniques.

These innovations appear to have continued with the conversion of the hospitals into trust status which triggered the creation of new financial and management accounting systems. Despite the abandonment of the internal market, pressure from the government to reduce costs and utilise resources more efficiently continues. Many finance departments seem to have found themselves on the receiving end of increasing demands for information to justify resource allocation and future cost pressures and as a result, in order to cope, they are adopting new accounting procedures.

Similarly in local authorities and government agencies, the main reason for adopting new practice is that of regulation and statute. In particular KPIs have been adopted across the board in local authorities as a result of the Best Value review process. This review, supplemented by other requests and recommendations from the Accounts Commission and the Scottish Executive, has driven much of the accounting innovation in the areas of government agencies and local authorities. As one financial manager stated:

New innovations are laid down by statute and quasi-statute eg Best Value Regimes.

Other changes have come as a result of problems arising from the re-organisation of local authorities. Units such as direct labour organisations have often greatly exceeded their budgets resulting in the imposition of ZBB. A few respondents in local government, however, appeared not to feel the direct pressure of legislation and regulation, but instead claimed that new accounting practices are adopted simply to comply with professional codes of accounting practice.

It is notable that little experimentation with accounting techniques in the public sector was reported in the survey. When accounting change does take place, it does so because it is forced by regulation, statute, or exhortation. Local authorities and government agencies appear to be heavily involved with innovative techniques in performance measurement and are showing reasonable interest in budgeting techniques, but it is only the healthcare sector that is showing strong involvement with all of these categories of accounting techniques. The results indicated that a few financial managers seem to have tried to adopt new systems without first being told that it is a good idea, although this does not seem to have happened in the healthcare sector where most of the accounting change has taken place. What this study does not show is how the regulators and statutory bodies acquire their knowledge about the best accounting techniques to use in particular circumstances. It is clear, however, that once directives are issued, changes are implemented and it is mainly the profession which provides the support that enables financial managers to acquire the necessary knowledge to implement the new systems. Nevertheless, these findings present a picture of somewhat limited innovation in accounting practices and, where there is change, this is essentially the result of externally-driven pressures. This lack of emphasis on innovation and new techniques is supportive of the findings discussed in chapter seven: techniques and practices would continue to be necessary for the public sector accountant of the future, but more importantly the 'softer' skills of management, of entrepreneurial thinking and human resource skills would be most necessary in future.

CHAPTER NINE

CONCLUSION

The public sector has attracted a great deal of attention from a variety of sources (policy-makers, the media, researchers and stakeholders) as it has undergone a sustained period of significant change. This research project has studied this phenomenon of change in the public sector from an accounting perspective. Its major purpose has been to explore the phenomenon of public sector change, both from the viewpoint of the significance or efficiency of specific accounting tools as mechanisms of change and also in the context of the impact of these changes to the public sector on the practices of accountants working within this sector of the economy.

This study examined four mechanisms of change: (1) the use of budgets, (2) VFM studies, (3) IT initiatives and (4) the use of management consultants (many of whom are accountants or are part of accounting firms) as agents of change. These choices of four dimensions of change reflect their importance in the literature. Each of these mechanisms was investigated in a different manner to obtain the best picture of their impact. For (1) detailed case studies were used; for (2) an expert group was the focus, supported by widely available data; (3) was based on government reports and (4) was based on interviews with management consultants.

The findings in this study show contrasting perspectives on the importance of these four mechanisms for change. As a context the researchers have used Costello's framework which categorises change states at three levels:

1. *developmental*, in which a specific new practice or technology is introduced.

2. *transitional*, in which new methods and techniques are aligned, with reorganisation of entities.
3. *transformational*, in which new structures and organisational change are combined with changes in strategy and vision.

The results of the investigation of the four change mechanisms identified in this study are shown in table 9.1

Table 9.1   Change states and change mechanisms: ex post appraisal

Change Mechansim / Change State	(1) Budgets	(2) VFM	(3) IT	(4) Management Consultants
1. Developmental	√	-	√	√
2. Transitional	-	√	-	√
3. Transformational	-	-	-	-

The evidence gathered as part of this study reaffirms the significance of the budget as a change mechanism in the public sector, but in a particular way. It has given accounting information visibility in addressing policy priorities and the effective management of resources. However, it can, on occasion, be seen as a blunt instrument rather than a sensitive management tool. This is a development tool which falls short of transformation, or even transition, in effecting change. In the study, the researchers have identified some problem areas in VFM audit relating to: (i) practical execution of VFM; (ii) the quality of evidence available to them; (iii) assessment issues; and, in particular, (iv) the problematic nature of 'quality'. However, there is sustained evidence in the literature which supports the view that VFM audits have been a key mechanism in achieving substantive change in the public sector in the past two decades. Nonetheless there are question marks over its continued role with the arrival of Best Value. There are also difficulties of addressing the more difficult and contentious issues of efficiency and effectiveness. In this way, VFM falls short of being a transformational mechanism. In a sense, the easier VFM exercises have been conducted in the earlier years of its life. Now the challenges are greater. Specifically, the researchers have identified the need for high level VFM studies of (1) IT initiatives in the public sector and (2) the use of management consultants in the public sector.

Also the findings are not indicative of management consultants as powerful change agents. Furthermore, on assessing the impact of these management consultants, the major frustration of consultancy in the public sector was that often their reports were not acted upon. The visibility of the management consultancy profession is not in doubt, but these findings suggest that a common view, namely that they are dominant in the transformation of the public sector, has to be regarded with some scepticism. They have had impact in a developmental sense and, to some extent, in effecting a transition of public sector organisations, but they fall far short of achieving transformation. The much vaunted reliance of government policy on IT initiatives as a mechanism for transforming the public sector does not appear warranted on the basis of the evidence presented in this study. There have been serial failures of extremely expensive, over-ambitious IT projects which were intended to make substantive change to the management of public services. At best, these schemes have assisted in the development of existing IT provision.

The second aspect of this study was the impact of changes within the public sector of the economy on the accountants who work in the public sector. This included an examination of the skills and competencies of the public sector accountant of the present and of the future which was based on the views of an expert group of leading public sector accountants. In addition, the researchers surveyed public sector accountants to get a picture of the range and types of techniques which were used to obtain a measure of the diffusion of accounting innovations.

The findings of this research on the competencies and skills of public sector accountants in this change era were based on interviews with members of an expert group of leading accountants in the public sector, who pointed to changing circumstances for the public sector accountant of the present and of the future. The traditional importance of the regularity function of accounting was likely to decline. Similarly the inward-looking focus on the management of best use of resources within the organisation was likely to decline. For the public sector accountant of the future, the role was seen as entrepreneurial, strategic and with a more significant liaison role than in the past. In terms of competencies, it was considered that traditional skills of communication, financial expertise and quantification would remain important. However, it was envisaged that increasingly the public sector accountant of the future would be required to have skills in marketing, human resources and general management. These results are consistent with the impact of the change mechanisms identified earlier: technologies and techniques are not, in themselves, enough to achieve change.

The results of the survey show that it is notable that little experimentation with accounting techniques in the public sector was reported. When accounting change does take place it takes place because it is forced by regulation, statute or exhortation. Local authorities and government agencies appear to be heavily involved with innovative techniques in performance measurement and are showing reasonable interest in reforming budgeting techniques, but it is only the healthcare sector that is showing strong involvement with all of these categories of accounting techniques. The results indicated that a few financial managers seem to have tried to adopt new systems without first being told that is a good idea, although this does not seem to have happened in healthcare sector where most of the accounting change has taken place. What this study does not show is how the regulators and statutory bodies acquire their knowledge about the best accounting techniques to use in particular circumstances. But it is clear that once directives are issued, changes are implemented and it is mainly the profession which provides the support that enables financial managers to acquire the necessary knowledge to implement the new systems. Nevertheless, these findings present a picture of somewhat limited innovation in accounting practices and, where there is change, this is essentially the result of externally-driven pressures. This lack of emphasis on innovation and new techniques is supportive of the findings discussed in chapter seven: techniques and practices would continue to be necessary for the public sector accountant of the future, but more importantly the 'softer' skills of management, of entrepreneurial thinking and human resource skills would be most necessary in future.

All of the above studies point to a continued turbulence for the public sector in the UK. However, this is an arena where there will continue to be a demand for accounting. This research suggests, though, that the public sector accountant of the future in the UK will be significantly different from the modern day equivalent. Changing circumstances, changing accounting and accountants, as the 'New Public Sector' becomes embedded in the economy.

In conclusion, on the basis of the findings contained in this report, the researchers make the following recommendations:

- there is a continuing need to develop budgetary systems in a way which links financial information to policy options and outcomes to bring to fruition the idea of policy-led budgets, particularly in local government;
- there is a history of budgetary initiatives which have not been successful in the health service. There is evidence presented here which suggests the manner, timing and trajectory of implementation are important factors in ensuring effectiveness of

budgetary systems and this more holistic and considered approach to budgetary design in health care is commended;

- VFM audits are now taken-for-granted mechanisms of scrutinising efficiency in public services. However, this study found that, in many cases, the more straightforward VFM studies had been undertaken and now VFM auditors were encountering more challenging studies. There is a need for a high level clarification of best practice for the new terrain in which VFM auditors find themselves in the 21st century. There is also a need for oversight bodies to review the role of VFM audit in relation to the Best Value regime;

- many IT initiatives within the public sector have failed, as evidence in this report shows. There is a growing awareness within the policy-making arena of the nature of this difficulty: but there is also a counter pressure to continue to use IT initiatives. There is a need for careful evaluation, not only of significant 'IT initiative' policies for public sector change, but also of the mechanisms of delivery and their project management to bring these projects to fruition;

- the role of management consultants as agents of change in the public sector has attracted a great deal of attention. However, on the basis of the findings in this report, a more careful evaluation of the use of management consultants by public sector organisations and the development of more effective central policies by government and/or oversight bodies on the effective use of management consultancy services is recommended;

- for the accounting professional bodies, with members in the public sector, there is a need for policies which recognise the shift in skills required to be successful accountants in the 'New Public Sector', with a move from traditional skills to new, 'softer' management skills. This is an issue for enhancing the competencies of existing accountants and development programmes for the accountants of the future in the public sector; and

- accountants in the public sector, public sector organisations and professional bodies need to re-examine the core technical competencies of the accountant in the non public sector, given the survey evidence of limited adoption of new accounting techniques, and the constraints on the adoption of such techniques.

REFERENCES

Brewer, J and A Hunter (1989), '*Multi-Method Research – A Synthesis of Styles*', Sage.

Brown, T (2001), 'Modernising the Public Sector: Technology as a Solution or a Problem', *Financial Accountability and Management*, Vol 17, No 4, November, pp.363-382.

Cabinet Office (1999), *Modernising Government*, HMSO.

Cabinet Office (2000), *Successful IT: Modernising Government in Action*, HMSO.

Clark, T and G Salaman (1996), 'The Management Guru as Organisational Witchdoctor', *Organisation Studies*, Vol 3(1), pp.85-107.

Committee of Public Accounts (2000), *Improving the Delivery of Government IT Projects*, First Report, Session 1999-2000, HMSO.

Costello, S J (1994), *Managing Change in the Workplace*, Irwin Professional Publishing.

CSSA (2001), "Getting IT Right for Government", www.cssa.co.uk/home/reports.

Denzin, N K (1978), *The Research Act*, Chicago, Aldine.

Efficiency Unit (1994), Cabinet Office, *The Government's Use of External Consultants*, HMSO.

Guthrie, J, O Olson and C Humphrey (1999), 'Debating Developments in New Public Financial Management: The Limits of Global Theorising and Some New Ways Forward', *Financial Accountability and Management*, Vol 15, Nos 3 and 4, pp 209-228.

Henley, D, A Likierman, J Perrin, M Evans, I Lapsley and J Whiteoak (1992), *Public Sector Accounting and Financial Control*, Chapman and Hall.

HM Government (1995), *Better Accounting for the Taxpayer's Money: The Government's Proposals*, Cm 2929, HMSO.

Labour Party (1997), *New Labour: Because Scotland Deserves Better*, London's Labour Party.

Lapsley, I (2001a), 'The Accounting-Clinical Interface – Implementing Budgets for Hospital Doctors', *Abacus*, Vol 37, No 1, February, pp 79-109.

Lapsley, I (2001b), 'Accounting, Modernity and Health Care Policy', *Financial Accountability and Management*, Vol 17, No 4, November, pp 331-350.

Lapsley, I and J Pallot (2000), 'Accounting, Management and Organizational Change: A Comparative Study of Local Government', *Management Accounting Research*, Vol 11, pp 213-229.

Lapsley, I and C Pong (2000), 'Modernisation versus Problematisation: Value-for-money Audit in Public Services', *European Accounting Review*, Vol 9, No 4, pp 541-567.

Lapsley, I and R Oldfield (2000), 'The Past is the Future: Constructing Public Sector Accountants', *Pacific Accounting Review*, Vol 11, No 2, January, pp 137-147.

Lapsley, I and R Oldfield (2001a), 'Transforming the Public Sector: Management Consultants as Agents of Change, *European Accounting Review*, Vol 10, No 3.

Lapsley, I and R Oldfield (2001b), 'The Accountant's Craft in the New Public Sector' *Irish Accounting Review*, Vol 8, No 1, Spring, pp 1-31.

Olson, O, J Guthrie and C Humphrey (eds) (1998), *Global Warning: Debating International Developments in New Public Management*, Cappelan Akademisk, Forlag, Oslo.

Osborne, D and T Gaebler (1992), *Reinventing Government*, Addison-Wesley.

Pollitt, C and G Bouckaert (2000), *Public Management Reform: A Comparative Analysis*, Oxford University Press.

Scottish Office (1997), *Best Value*, SODD Circular 22/97, Local Government Group, Edinburgh.

Scottish Office (1998), *Best Value*, SODD Circular 12/98, Local Government Group, Edinburgh.

Smith, H W (1975), *Strategies of Social Research – The Methodological Imagination*, Prentice-Hall.

Wallander, J (1999), 'Budgeting – An Unnecessary Evil', *Scandinavian Journal of Management*, Vol 15, pp 405-421.

APPENDIX 1

Management Consultancy Practices in the Public Sector: Interview Checklist

1. Which parts of the public sector have you worked within, and what type of work have you done?

2. Generally, do you believe that your work has been successful? Can you think of any specific successes or difficulties that stand out? (For example, instances when your recommendations were not put into practice).

3. What are the principal skills/expertise which consultants use to help public sector organisations?

4. How would you describe the relationship that you have with the client organisation?

5. Do you foresee more work for consultants in the public sector in the future? Please give examples.

6. What is your view on the current situation within the public sector, compared with when you first worked within it? Please give examples.

    (a) is there a more visible finance role?
    (b) is management stronger (*vis à vis* other professionals)?
    (c) is the public sector now more business like?
    (d) have public sector organisations become more flexible and less standardised?
    (e) is there scope for further downsizing in public sector organisations?
    (f) how does the culture of public sector organisations compare to private sector organisations, with which you are familiar?
    (g) are public sector organisations responsive to private sector ideas?

APPENDIX 2

1. From the list below, please tick the accounting techniques which are used, or have been used (within the last 10 years), within your organisation. Could you also please indicate in which areas of the organisation they are used, when they were introduced and, if applicable, when they were taken out of use.

Budgeting Techniques:

Zero Based Budgeting	
Resource Management	
Activity Based Management	

Costing Techniques:

Target Costing	
Activity Based Costing	
Strategic Cost Management	

Performance Measurement Techniques:

Functional Analysis	
Key Performance Indicators	
Balanced Scorecard	

2. When were the accounting techniques which are used (or have been used previously within your organisation) introduced? For example, was there a specific event that triggered their introduction?

3. If a particular technique(s) is no longer in use, why was it discarded?

4. How does your organisation keep up to date with innovations in accounting techniques?

5. Which of the above techniques was/are used within your organisation have been the most successful? Why?

6. Does your organisation have a system for monitoring the use/ effectiveness of accounting techniques? Please describe.

7. What contribution do non-financial managers make to the development of accounting techniques?